THE NEW RELIGIOUS WORLD

Anne Bancroft

HODDER
Wayland

an imprint of Hodder Children's Books

Editor
Peter Harrison
Managing Editor
Belinda Hollyer
Design
Sally Boothroyd
Picture Rescarch
Caroline Mitchell
Production
Rosemary Bishop
Factual Consultant
Dr. Owen Cole

We are grateful for the assistance of the Watch Tower Bible and Tract Society, London.

First published in paperback in Great Britain in 1992 by Simon & Schuster Young Books

Revised and updated in 2001 by Hodder Wayland, an imprint of Hodder Children's Books

© Hodder Wayland 1992

Hodder Children's Books
A division of Hodder Headline Ltd
338 Euston Road
London NW1 3BH

Printed and bound in Hong Kong

ISBN 0 7502 3324 9

Cover pictures: top, The Mormon Tabernacle Choir; **centre top,** A Rastafarian father and child; **centre bottom,** Hare Krishnas beating drums and cymbals in the street; **left,** The Reverend Moon blessing newly married couples; **right,** daily life in a Rajneesh community.

Endpapers: Followers of the Hare Krishna movement displaying their *mantra* at the base of Nelson's Column during a large meeting in London's Trafalgar Square.

Title page: Rajneeshis practising Dynamic Meditation. They are wearing lockets which contain a picture of the *Bhagwan* Shree Rajneesh.

Contents page: A European woman wearing Indian dress and nose jewellery gives a traditional palms-together Indian greeting.

Contents

Introduction
A time of change

Below right: A West Indian family arriving in Britain during the 1950s. Many West Indians were encouraged to emigrate to Britain during this period, by promises of employment. West Indians brought their culture and beliefs with them to their new homes.

Below left: A European woman reading and holding prayer beads among Tibetans. Many Europeans looked to the East for a new religious direction, from the late 1960s onward. They travelled in large numbers to India and other Eastern countries.

Since the second half of the twentieth century the Western world has begun to pay attention to many new spiritual ideas. People of other races have come to live in Western countries and have brought their beliefs and practices with them. Their attitudes have given new insights to Westerners and brought about many changes in the Western understanding of religion. Some of these changes can be seen in schools. Morning assemblies may now include readings from the scriptures of different religions, as well as selections from their hymns, prayers and stories.

The new 'awakening'
Some groups of people have also started to look at their own religions and have developed new beliefs about them. Sometimes they call it a new 'awakening'. They try to understand their

religion in a fresh way. Often they feel a deep need for the meaning of religion to become clear to them, and they long to experience a fresh way of seeing. Consequently a number of new 'faiths' have sprung up.

Most of them have certain things in common. Their followers believe that a spiritual experience is the most important event; that it changes the person and leads directly to being wise and creating a good world. The followers are usually young people who want to make a peaceful and happy world to live in.

Difficult relationships
In the past, new religious movements have caused a lot of troubled feelings in the communities where they grew up. Parents have often become alarmed when they saw

their son or daughter turn away from them to follow a different religious path. Some of the new 20th century groups in particular are upsetting to parents, because they seem to insist on a way of life which young people are forced to follow. This forced way of life has been called 'brainwashing' by those who are against these groups, and they have accused the groups of breaking up families and controlling young people's minds. Some parents have been persuaded to pay large sums of money to people who will kidnap their son or daughter and stop the control of their minds.

What this book sets out to do

This book is not about whether people are right or wrong to join new religious groups, nor is it about whether the new religious movements themselves are 'right' or 'wrong'.

Each group has its own history, beliefs and customs and these are described as clearly as possible in the pages which follow. A member of each group has been asked to reply to common criticisms of their beliefs, so that a complete picture can be given.

It may be asked why these particular groups were chosen. Very simply, they are the ones people hear most about. They make a point of meeting the public, and so are the ones people are most likely to read about or see on television.

Nothing remains changeless, least of all religion. When a new faith appears, it need not so much threaten old faiths as renew them with youth and strength. That can't happen unless the new faith is given attention and listened to. This book is a way of giving attention to the new faiths.

Mormons
Joseph Smith's struggles

The Church of Jesus Christ of Latter-Day Saints, known today as the Mormon Church, was begun by a man called Joseph Smith, in North America, in 1830. As a boy of 14 Joseph was confused by the many different religious sects (groups) springing up at that time, and he went alone into the woods to ask God for advice. He later told his followers that both God and Jesus appeared to him there, advising him not to to join any existing church but to prepare himself for important work ahead. When Joseph was 18 an angel whom he called Moroni appeared to him while he was praying, telling him that there was a book written on pages of gold hidden in a hill nearby. Four years later the angel told Joseph how to find the book. It was written in Hebrew, and Joseph began to translate it into English.

The Book of Mormon
The pages of the book told the story of two tribes of Israelites who came to South America almost 4000 years ago. It said in the book that Jesus Christ came to South America after his resurrection, and established a period of peace among the people living there. This peace was later destroyed by sin. A great battle took place in which the good people were defeated. The leader of the good people was called Mormon. Before he was killed, he gave his son Moroni a golden book which told the story of what had happened. Moroni hid the book and waited for instructions from God before he told Joseph Smith where it was, almost 1400 years later.

The persecutions
When he had finished translating the Book of Mormon, Joseph began preaching, and soon attracted followers, but he also met with opposition from other people. The church moved from the state of Ohio to Missouri, but there it met a great deal of trouble and after a battle in which 17 Mormons, including children, were killed, the church moved on to Illinois. There the Mormons built a city which they called Nauvoo. Nauvoo expanded, but its very strength and prosperity brought trouble again from its neighbours. They were particularly disturbed by the Mormon custom of a man taking several wives. Some Mormons also objected to this, and started a rival Mormon group. Joseph Smith's followers smashed their rivals' printing press and both sides took up arms. The Governor of Illinois

Below: The Tabernacle, or meeting-house, in Salt Lake City, the world headquarters of the Mormon Church. The Mormon Tabernacle Choir performs in this building, and large meetings are also held there.

Left: A stained glass window in a Mormon church showing the vision of God and Jesus which came to Joseph Smith at the age of 14. He had gone into a wood to try and clear his mind of the confusion caused by different religious ideas.

promised Joseph that if he would surrender peacefully he would be guaranteed safe conduct out of the state. Joseph gave himself up and was put in jail. On 27 June 1844 the jail was attacked by 150 men, and Joseph and his brother were shot and killed.

What happened next

A year later Brigham Young, the president of the Mormon's highest council, was chosen to take Joseph's place. But the persecution continued and the Mormons decided to leave Illinois. They began migrating 1300 miles westwards, in covered wagons or on foot, through wild country to the edge of the Great Salt Lake in what is now Utah.

During the next four years some 80000 families went there, and the route they travelled is now known as the Mormon Trail. They built Salt Lake City to Joseph Smith's plans and communities grew up around it. After arguments with the government Utah became the 45th state of the USA in 1896. Since then the Mormons have lived in peace.

Mormons
Living as a Saint

All Mormons are called Saints. Children become Saints around the age of eight, when they are baptized by total immersion. Young men and women spend 18 months to two years in missionary work. Men and women are expected to become good husbands and wives when they marry. There are about five million Mormons in the world and each working adult gives one tenth of their income to the church.

What Mormons believe

To the Mormons, Joseph Smith is their prophet, and so they have no doubt about what he said. They believe that he rediscovered God's plan for the human race which had been lost for centuries because of human foolishness. This is God's plan for people: to work hard, to civilise the wilderness, and to prepare for the return of Jesus. Mormons believe that God, Jesus, the Holy Spirit and

Above: Three priests of the Mormon Church welcome a young man into the priesthood. All boy Mormons join the Mormon priesthood at the age of 12. There are two kinds of priesthood in the Mormon Church, the Aaronic priesthood and the Melchizedek priesthood. Children become members of the Aaronic priesthood, but only adults can become Melchizedek priests.

Right: A Mormon baptism in progress. Both people are standing waist deep in water. The person baptising has his right arm raised. He first says the name of the person to be baptized. Then he says, ''Having been commissioned by Jesus Christ, I baptize you . . .'' and gives the person their baptismal name. The person being baptized is then put completely under water for a few seconds. When he comes out of the water again he will have been 'reborn' into the Mormon Church.

Satan are physically real, and that human beings actually look like God. Humans have immortal souls and can obtain a place in the highest of several heavens if they do good with God's gift of free will.

Daily Life

Mormons do not drink alchohol, tea or coffee and they do not smoke. But singing and dancing are encouraged since God created humans to be joyful. Meetings for worship are simple in style and the main services are on Sunday. Mormons usually fast on the first Sunday of every month.

Baptism of the dead

Mormons believe that it is possible to baptize their dead relatives and so allow them to enter heaven. So Mormons trace back their ancestors all over the world as far into the past as they can. Records are kept of all these ancestors in enormous vaults in the Utah mountains, and are available to Mormons everywhere.

Women and marriage

Women cannot become priests. Marriage to a good Saint is the only way a woman can gain entry to the highest heaven. Indeed, Mormons believe that no-one, man or woman, can enter heaven unless they are married. Women must be obedient to their husbands and dress modestly.

Mormons believe that marriage is for eternity and that families reunite after death. They also believe that there is a life in heaven before birth, and so every married couple has a duty to produce as many children as possible in order to give earthly life to souls waiting in heaven to be born.

Above: A Mormon Sunday school in Western Samoa. The teacher is showing the children a picture of the angel Moroni appearing to Joseph Smith. The Church of Latter-Day Saints has many missionaries in Polynesia, and it sees Polynesians as a lost tribe of Israel. There is also a large Mormon University in Hawaii.

Misunderstandings

Mormon men have several wives.

"The Church does not allow men to have more than one wife any longer. Several people within the last two years have been told they must leave the Church for doing just that. At the time when Brigham Young was our prophet, it was the custom for a man to support a number of wives so that large families could be raised. But now Mormons honour the laws of their countries."

Joseph Smith is worshipped as a God.

"Joseph Smith is honoured as our first prophet but we have never worshipped him. Jesus Christ is the head of our Church and it is him we worship."

Mormons are racially prejudiced, and think of American Indians as an inferior people.

"The Lamanites, as Mormons call American Indians, are not inferior and are always treated equally by Mormons. I had a Navajo foster son, and saw him as my own."

Rastafarians
Jah for I

The original Rastafarians were Jamaicans led by a man called Marcus Garvey. They believed that the coronation of Ras Tafari (Prince of the Tafari family) Haile Selassie as Emperor of Ethiopia in 1930 fulfilled a Biblical prophecy. They accepted him as the living God, and Ethiopia as the promised land to which they would return. Many black people now share this belief, although there are still less than one million actual Rastafarians.

The spread of Rastafarianism

The Rastafarians became established in Britain during the 1970s. Most young members came from Jamaica as immigrants with their parents from 1960 onwards. Young Rastas (a shortened name for Rastafarians) believe their parents to have been betrayed into leaving their homeland in Jamaica for a new life, only to be rejected by British society. They will not accept the same rejection. They have turned against many of their parents' beliefs, refusing to go to church or share their Christian ideas, but instead building a religious attitude of their own. They accept some of the laws of the country where they live, but not all of them. One said: "I and I obey God's law, basic human truths and rights; not the law of the Queen of England." This has sometimes meant conflict with the British police.

Rastafarian beliefs

Rastafarian beliefs are based on the Bible. Many Rastas believe it is an account of Rastafarian history. Rastas believe they are Israelites, because they believe that when the 12 tribes of Israel were scattered, the spirit of the Lord went into Ethiopia – and thus Ethiopians became the Chosen People of the Israelites. They became scattered as a people when black Africans were taken from Africa, as slaves.

The Exile

The countries to which Africans were taken as slaves (Europe, America and the West Indies) are seen as places of exile. Rastas call them 'Babylon', after the city in the Bible where the Israelite people were taken as prisoners. Rastas see Babylon civilisation as corrupt and destructive, persuading black people to think of themselves as inferior to those who are not black, and also to believe in Christianity. Christianity is seen as being deceitful, since it preaches a God who is not black.

Prayer

God is called '*Jah*' and families pray daily to *Jah* Haile Selassie. They come together for communal prayers, singing, drumming and preaching at informal meetings in the house of a leader. There are no churches. Sometimes there is a *Nyabingi*, a great get-together of many Rastas. Before meetings people fast and purify themselves. Self-discipline such as fasting is thought essential to the deep search within themselves which every person must

Below: A Rastafarian artist at work in Jamaica carving a figure out of wood. He has put his pencil into his hair for convenience. Such work helps Rastafarians to try and live without being dependent on Babylon. In the background is a painting of Haile Selassie.

make. They should wait quietly for the call from *Jah* which will direct them. The most important teaching is 'peace and love'.

I and I

For Rastas there is no God outside themselves, for God the Father is within them. They believe that God always spoke of himself as 'I'. So when Rastas talk of themselves they say 'I and I', meaning their true nature as God and themselves. 'I and I' is a way of using words to make this idea of oneness clear. So when Rastafarians speak of themselves as 'I' they

mean it in a sense of a total uplifting of themselves. Addressing another Rastafarian they say 'I am I' – this means the oneness of two persons. 'I and I' means that God is within all people.

Reincarnation

Rastas do not believe that death takes place and many do not believe that Haile Selassie has died. When death does occur it is often seen as a trick of Babylon. It is believed that the spirit of the dead person will resist the trickery and be reincarnated elsewhere.

Above: A group of Rastafarian drummers. They live in one of the parts of Kingston, Jamaica where reggae and Rastafarianism began. Some Rastafarians, such as the man on the left of this photograph, believe they must cover their heads at all times.

15

Rastafarians
Rasta talk

Rastafarians spend many hours discussing the Bible and its meaning. They believe there is no one meaning, and all opinions are respected. Talk on any deep subject such as the Bible is called 'reasoning'.

Reggae is inseparable from Rastafarianism. Deprived of their own culture and language by slavery, Rastas see their music as the mark of their identity. It expresses the true Rastaman, and the secret of its rhythms is kept from non-Rastafarians. The words of reggae songs describe Rastafarian beliefs and sufferings. It is said to be "a music of blood, black-reared, pain-rooted, heart-geared". Before he died Bob Marley was seen as the most important person in reggae music.

I-tal
Rastas follow very strict rules about what they eat and drink. No rum, milk or coffee may be drunk, only fruit juice. They do not smoke tobacco. All food is carefully prepared with great cleanliness. Rastas are mainly vegetarian and do not eat pork, shellfish, or any fish over 18 cm long. They do not add salt to their food. So *I-tal* means food that is natural and clean.

Going to school
Rastas do not like their children to attend ordinary schools, believing that what they are taught is untrue and immoral. In some places, Haile Selassie schools are being set up with the help of the Ethiopian Orthodox Church.

The Lion of Judah
Rastas believe that Haile Selassie, Lion of Judah, united the human and the animal world. He was fearless, and lions roamed his garden and slept at his feet. The proud walk of the lion is copied by Rastamen, and a lion symbol is featured on many Rastafarian objects.

Dreadlocks and colours
A number of Rastafarians believe they should not cut their hair or beards because a verse in the Bible tells them not to. They put their hair into unusual shapes called dreadlocks, to show other people that they are Rastafarians.

Red, yellow and green woollen hats worn by young Rastamen are to be seen in most big cities. Their significance is: red for the blood of

Right: This Rastafarian's dreadlocks look very long beside the short hair of the children around him. Rastafarians follow the passage in the Bible which says: "They shall not make baldness upon their head, neither shall they shave off the corner of their beard . . ." (Leviticus Ch.21, v.5). Instead of cutting their hair, they twist it into shapes which are meant to make people feel respect and awe for them. The Rastafarian name for this respect is 'dread', which is why they call this kind of hair 'dreadlocks'.

Left: Rastafarians at the famous annual carnival in the Notting Hill district of London. Every year thousands of West Indians living in London hold this summer festival and Rastafarians attend it too.

Below: The funeral of the reggae singer, Bob Marley. This hill in Jamaica is covered with people who have come to mourn. There was great grief among Rastafarians when Marley died.

martyrs and slaves, yellow for the Rastafarian faith and for Jamaica, and green for Ethiopia.

The Return

There have been times when Rastafarians in Jamaica thought they would be able to go back to Africa, but very few have gone. Part of being a Rastafarian is waiting for the return. Nowadays, young Rastas see Ethiopia and Africa as more of an idea, like heaven.

Misunderstandings

Rastafarianism is not a real religion.

"It is a true religion, revealed by Marcus Garvey in Jamaica. Marcus Garvey was the reincarnation of the prophet John the Baptist. He made black people realise their black mentality. He prophesied the coming of Haile Selassie, because he said that black people must look through the spectacles of Ethiopia for their God and King."

Rastafarians have no culture.

"The reason is because black people have entered the wilderness and lost themselves and become dead. They are slaves, and everything that is negative. Before we can return unto our God, *Jah* Rastafari, black men and women must be reborn.

Rastafarians do not like working.

"We like to work, but the people we work for object to our customs. We do not cut our hair and we must always cover it, men and women. Women can work because nobody minds a headscarf, but because they wear hats, Rasta men are not wanted."

Unification Church ('Moonies')
The Reverend Moon

In 1920 Sun Myung Moon was born in what is now North Korea. When he was 16 years old he had a vision, in which Jesus Christ appeared to him on a mountainside. During the next nine years, while becoming an engineer in Japan, Moon studied the Bible deeply. He received in visions the main teaching of The Divine Principle, the basic scripture of his church. In 1946 Moon left his Japanese university to go home to Korea and spread his message. But he was seized by the Korean police, beaten up, tortured, and thrown out in the snow. Some of his followers rescued him.

After some months he started to teach again but was arrested once more, and sentenced to work in a labour camp.

After three gruelling years in the labour camp Moon was freed by United Nations army forces. He then walked and bicycled the long distance to Pusan in South Korea, carrying on his back another prisoner who had been freed with a broken leg. After he arrived in Pusan, Moon built his first church there out of tin cans and cardboard boxes. In 1954 he officially founded the Unification Church. The Church now has 4.5 million members,

Right: The Reverend Moon and his wife with eight of their children. The Reverend Moon has now handed over leadership of the Church to his third son, Hyun-Jin Moon, and his wife, Jun-Sook Moon. However, Reverend Moon is still an important figure in the Church.

Below: A Moonie mass wedding. It took place in Madison Square Gardens, New York in 1982, and 2075 couples were married.

often known as 'Moonies', and it belongs to a much bigger group of churches called the Family Federation for World Peace and Unification.

What the Moonies believe

Building a moral society is the most important belief for Moonies. Both scientific ideas and religion should be used to remove spiritual and physical ignorance, which they believe has prevented people from creating this kind of society. Moonies see themselves as having three main aims:

* The creation of God-centred families as a foundation for a moral and healthy society.
* The creation of one human family going beyond race or nationality and centred on God's love.
* The creation of a God-centred society concerned with social issues.

God as Father is very real to Unificationists, and they have frequent visions. They believe that God's original plan was for men and women to have a perfect relationship with him, loving each other eternally in marriage and also as brothers and sisters. The Unification Church is dedicated to removing hatred and prejudice on the grounds of race, nationality or class from the world. They believe that Communists are inspired by Satan, but are willing to try to convert them.

The Divine Principle

Moonies believe the Divine Principle is God's law, which has been present throughout the history told in the Bible. God created the human race in Adam (the first man). Adam sinned against God, and this has affected all his descendants. In order to restore goodness to people God sent a second Adam – Jesus – in whom the new humanity is still to be created, since Jesus was prematurely killed. In order for the new humanity to come into being, people must join the new family of Jesus Christ and leave behind the old family of Adam. This requires a 'new birth' and a new father.

Sung Sang and Hyung Sang

Moonies also believe that God and all humanity are made up of two things: of *Sung Sang*, which means inner thoughts and *Hyung Sang*, which means outside shape. *Sung Sang* is closer to God because it is nearer the heart.

Below: A mass meeting under a banner which says 'The New Future of Christianity'. Hanging above the crowd is the symbol of the Unification Church. The circle in the centre represents God, and the 12 rays coming from the centre are the 12 gates to the new life. The arrows encircling the symbol are the give and take relationship between God and people, which Moonies believe is the basis for unity in the world.

Unification Church ('Moonies')
Disordered love

Moonies believe that Adam's sin against God was one of self-love. They believe that human love is 'disordered' because it is self-centred, and this affects all human love. For this reason they believe the key to salvation is creating love which is centred upon God. This includes God-centred sexual love, leading to God-centred children. For this reason marriage is particularly important to Moonies.

Mass weddings
Arranged marriages are usual in the East, and church leaders act as parents in arranging marriages. Reverend Moon and his wife still arrange some marriages themselves, especially between second-generation Moonies, who have been church members all their lives. The marriages frequently join together people of different races. No-one is forced to be married, and if they don't like their suggested partner they can say 'No'. Only those couples who have served for several years in the church can take part in the large weddings. Since marriage

is for God and not for the individual, the couples are married in an impersonal setting. At the ceremony the couples are asked to remember two things:
• The marriage is for eternity and not just until the couple die.
• They should educate their children to become morally excellent.

Communities
Many younger Moonies live in communities with a 'captain' as head. They give all the money they earn to the community and take back what they need, such as money for a pair of shoes. Meals and a room to stay in are paid for by the community.

People live together as brothers and sisters, and do not have sexual relationships before they marry. Husbands and wives do not expect to live together completely until they have children. They will go wherever the church feels they are needed, even if this means being separated for a time. The Reverend Moon and

Right: The 'Little Angels' of Korea. They are members of the Unification Church who perform traditional Korean dances. They travel all over the world giving performances and earning money to help the church.

his wife are thought of as their father and mother.

Daily life
Moonies get early to pray and sing together before the day's work. Some sell flowers on the streets of big cities. Others will 'witness' from door to door, or set up a table of literature at a street corner. Many work in businesses owned by the church. Others work preparing the big religious conferences organised by the Unification Church in many countries throughout the year.

Running businesses
The church is supported partly by businesses which it owns in Japan, Korea, the USA and Uraguay. The church also owns several daily newspapers, as well as magazines and a hi-tech company specializing in computer-aided design. It is also involved in shipbuilding and fish-processing companies, and has recently opened a car factory in North Korea. It uses income from these businesses to fund charity projects in the community.

Misunderstandings

The Unification Church kidnaps young people, and controls their minds.

"People study our teaching, and they often come closer to God, and want to give their lives to doing God's will. Then they join our movement which is similar to a religious order. Parents have joined too."

Moonies break up families and stop parents seeing children.

"We try very hard to improve our relations with our families. Many people, however, do not understand our faith and how much it means to us."

Moonies do not meet their marriage partners until their wedding day.

"This is not true. In reality a large number of people meet in a big room. Reverend Moon is guided by God to choose marriage partners among them. Then, each selected couple leaves the room to decide whether to agree to marry or not. If either do not want it, they go back to the room and new partners are chosen. If they accept, they bow to Reverend Moon and become engaged for up to three years before they marry."

Above: Here, some American Moonies are helping to clean the streets. This is one of the many community projects organized by the church to give support to all the people in a particular community, including those who are not members of the church.

21

Transcendental Meditation
The nature of mind

Right: Maharishi Mahesh Yogi visiting his British TM headquarters at the end of 1984. He loves to be surrounded by flowers and always has many arranged around him at public meetings.

Below: The effects of Transcendental Meditation can be measured in brain-waves. Scientists like the one shown in this picture spend a great deal of time investigating the effects of TM on the body and mind.

Maharishi Mahesh Yogi is an Indian *guru*, or holy man. He has long hair and a long beard, wears a white robe, and often carries a flower. He is a Hindu (a follower of a traditional Indian religion) who has discovered a way of meditation practice for Westerners.

How TM began

Maharishi studied physics as a young man at an Indian university. While he was there he met a famous spiritual teacher called Guru Dev. He worked and studied with Guru Dev for 13 years. When Guru Dev died, Maharishi went to live alone in a cave in the Himalayas. After two years of silence he came back to the world with the belief that life should be lived in happiness, and so he began to teach TM. To begin with, he founded his own school of meditation at a place in northern India called Rishikesh. Rishikesh is a Hindu holy place where the river Ganges flows down out of the Himalayas.

After that Maharishi travelled around the world and taught TM wherever he went. The technique has so far been learned by over four million people all over the world, including almost 200,000 in Britain. It is used in

schools, businesses, and even prisons in many countries. TM does not involve changes in lifestyle or belief and so is popular with many different kinds of people.

The practice

Maharishi has said that TM is an easy technique which anyone can do anywhere. At a private interview a teacher gives a word, known as a *mantra*, to the student. It is personal to the student. It is ever written down, never repeated to anyone else, but just thought of in the mind. Students meditate for 20 minutes at a time, repeating their *mantra* to themselves. The technique itself involves no special effort or concentration. The word itself is a sound without any particular meaning – a proper word, it is thought, would keep the mind too active.

The effects

Maharishi believes that TM helps people to make full use of the energy, intelligence, and happiness that exists within everyone. TM, he says, allows the mind naturally and effortlessly to settle to quieter levels of thinking until it 'transcends', or goes beyond, thought. Maharishi describes this as the state of 'pure conscious-

ness', in which the mind is calm and peaceful, yet fully awake inside. Medical tests have shown that people need to breathe in 20% less oxygen during TM. The heartbeat, pulse, and breathing rate slow down, which brings the effect of complete relaxation. This deep rest seems to refresh the whole person, and leads to increased energy and enthusiasm.

The purpose of life

Maharishi believes that the purpose of life is the expansion of happiness. Practising Transcendental Meditation is the first step to achieving this goal. He believes that an intelligence greater than ours has caused the world to exist. People's minds are part of this greater intelligence. When they are in the state of transcendence they can feel this.

What people usually think of as their minds is really only on the surface, full of thoughts. When thoughts disappear, the mind becomes still and can experience the larger mind. From there it can return to everyday life refreshed. Maharishi believes, and research indicates, that if only 1% of humanity practised this way of meditation there would be peace and harmony throughout the world.

Below: Mentmore Towers, where Maharishi Foundation had its UK headquarters from 1979 to 1999. Maharishi Foundation was established to help co-ordinate the effects of harmony and happiness which Maharishi and his followers believe can be achieved by practising TM.

Transcendental Meditation
Awareness

Lifestyle
People do not have to alter their lifestyle in any way when learning TM. Maharishi leaves it up to individuals to decide how to live, though he does encourage vegetarianism. He believes that the practice of TM will lead to a better way of life anyway. He does not think that enjoyment should be given up but that life should be spiritually richer.

The great mistake
Maharishi believes that many people are mistaken when they think that awareness of a greater mind is impossible in ordinary life. He says firmly that life should not be split into the transcendental and the everyday. Sharing in the greater intelligence which made the world should instead be brought into ordinary life.

Advanced practices
After practising Transcendental Meditation regularly twice a day for six months, it is possible to take an advanced course, called the TM-*Sidhi* programme. *Sidhi* is an Indian word meaning an unusual power. Maharishi believes that anything is possible when a person's awareness has grown. He has found a way which he believes allows people to develop such unusual powers as rising from the ground, seeing into the future, subduing hunger and thirst, seeing where lost objects are, and looking into one's own body. He calls this way *samyama*. A person must be in a special state of mind, between the stillness of TM and the first movement of thought in their minds. If a person is properly aware at that point, then they can use the *sidhis* correctly.

Where to learn
Maharishi has established TM centres in almost every country in the world. Roydon Hall in Kent is the headquarters of the organisation in Britain. There are teachers in most of the main towns and cities around the country. Altogether there are about 40,000 teachers around the world.

The Age of Enlightenment
In 1975 Maharishi announced the 'Age of Enlightenment'. This will be a time when people all over the world become happier as a result of TM being practised in the cities and towns where they live.

Above: People in the United States practising TM. The usual position for meditation is sitting comfortably in a chair. These meditators are part of a programme designed to help people suffering from ill-health, including the effects of age.

Below: This group of American children attended a school founded by Maharishi. The school is part of the Maharishi University of Management in Iowa, United States. There is a Maharishi School in Lancashire in the UK where all the children and teachers practise TM together at the start of each day.

Baha'is
Baha'u'llah

In first half of the 19th century, there was a holy man in Persia (now called Iran) called the *Bab*. He said he was the teacher of a new message from God, and that a greater prophet than himself would come after him. He gave new meaning to the Islamic laws and ceremonies in Persia of prayer, fasting, marriage, divorce and inheritance. He constantly praised and longed for the next prophet, and believed that person would appear after his own death.

As the *Bab's* teaching spread he came to be feared by the ruler of Persia, and was imprisoned. His followers were persecuted and the *Bab* himself was executed in 1850. Two years later two of his followers tried to assassinate the Shah (the ruler of Persia). In the violence which came after, many of his followers were put in prison, including the most devoted of them all, a man called Baha'u'llah. After some months Baha'u'llah was released, but had all his wealth taken away from him. He travelled on foot to Baghdad (in modern Iraq). But in spite of such persecution, he continued the *Bab's* work. He became the centre and real founder of the Baha'i religion.

Right: The last great leader of the Baha'i faith, 'Abd'ul Baha, who died in Haifa in 1921. He spent the last 8 years of his life in what is now the modern state of Israel. He worked for the peace of that region, and his life was frequently in danger.

Identity for Baha'is
In 1868 Baha'u'llah introduced the Baha'i greeting – *Allah-u-Abha* ('God is All Glorious'), and at the same time people began to call his followers Baha'is. After all his suffering, Baha'u'llah was able to live in peace at the end of his life. He died in 1892.

His son, 'Abdu'l Baha, took over as leader of the Baha'is. He also faced persecution, sometimes from people who were members of his own family. In the early 20th century he travelled to Britain and America, founding Baha'i groups wherever he went, and died in 1921.

Haifa
Baha'u'llah visited Haifa (in modern Israel) four times in the last years of his life. He showed 'Abdu'l Baha where the *Bab's* body should be buried, on the rocky hillside of Mount Carmel. There is a shrine there now with gardens. Haifa is a holy place of pilgrimage for Baha'is.

Religions and prophets
Baha'is believe that all religions are divine. A human being through whom God speaks is rare, so only the names of a few are known; Baha'u'llah is the latest of such people to be born.

His mission was to bring peace to the world, uniting all races and religions. He believed that people cannot understand God on their own but can learn about him through the founders of religions. Baha'is believe that all religions are like chapters in a book. There will be more chapters to come, and another great prophet will be born in 1000 years. In the Baha'i view, each religion prepares the way for the next one, and religions find new ways of saying what the old ones taught.

The soul
Each soul comes into existence at conception and is unique. A soul needs to be born into a human body to learn to develop love and truthfulness. These will be needed after death, and so the soul must develop them here on earth, just as a child develops arms and legs in the womb.

Heaven and hell
Baha'is see these not as places, but as states of being. Heaven is being near to God, and hell is being far away from him. So when the body dies, it is not something to be afraid of but something to look forward to. It is a birth into a fuller life.

The force of good
There is only one force in the universe, Baha'is believe, and that is the force of good. Evil is the absence of good, just as darkness is the absence of light. Even desires are right if meant for the good of other people, and to help them draw nearer to God.

Above: The entrance to the tomb of Baha'u'llah in Haifa, Israel. The shoes in the foreground have been left by a person who has entered the tomb to pay respect to Baha'u'llah's teaching.

Baha'is
Citizens of the world

Baha'is see themselves as world citizens, who believe that loyalty should be directed towards the planet we live on rather than to individual nations. They call themselves a World Community. They never use armed force in their own interests, and have remained defenceless when attacked, as in Iran. They believe that for every Baha'i killed because of being a Baha'i, another 100 people join the movement.

Daily life

There are now three and a half million Baha'is in the world. They say either a short, medium or long prayer every day. They do not drink alcohol or take drugs. All Baha'is are considered teachers, and so there are no ministers or clergy. They are all expected to spread the teaching of their faith wherever possible. In order to draw nearer to God, Baha'is between the ages of 15 and 70 do not eat or drink between the hours of sunrise and sunset, from the 2nd to the 20th March every year.

A single life is not encouraged and marriage is seen as being very important. Sexual relationships outside marriage are not allowed and divorce is frowned on. Baha'is may choose a partner from any race or religion.

The place of women

Baha'i women and men are completely equal. Baha'u'llah laid down that women should be educated to the same standard as men. If a family does not have enough money to educate all the children, the girls are given priority because of their importance as future mothers.

The Baha'i calendar

There are 19 months in the Baha'i calendar, each of them being 19 days long. On the first day of the month there is a '19 Day Feast' when the local Spiritual Assembly consults with its community. Only registered Baha'is may be present. Babies and children can attend if they have been registered by their parents, but at the age of 15 all children must assume Baha'i responsibilities. They cannot attend the feast if they do not want to take on these responsibilities.

New Year is 21 March; 21 April, called the Ridvan Festival, is the celebration of the

Below: A festival taking place outside a Baha'i house of worship in Samoa. Europeans and Samoan Baha'is join in celebrating this happy occasion. Although the 9-sided design is always used, the buildings vary in their appearance from one country to another.

Left: This group of Baha'is have made a float and joined in a local festival in London. The two doves on the globe in the float represent the Baha'i belief in world peace.

Below: Here Baha'i children of many countries sing together. They have met at a conference in Ireland, of Baha'is from all over the world. In the background is the symbol of the Baha'i faith, the 9-pointed star.

announcement by Baha'u'llah's followers that they believed God spoke to them through him.

Places of worship

A completed House of Worship must be nine-sided and domed, with its doors open to people of all races. Chanting is allowed but no musical instruments. At present there are only five such houses, but many more are planned.

Misunderstandings

All Baha'is are Muslims.

"The faith began in a Muslim country, but we are as independent from the Muslims as the Christians are from the Jews. We have our own holy book, the Book of Laws (Kitabi Aqdas), and calendar."

Baha'is can work miracles because many of them are spiritual healers.

"Abdu'l-Baha said if a strong person concentrated their mind on a sick person and was certain that a cure would take place, an 'excitement of the nerves' would be produced in the sick person and he or she would recover from their illness. Baha'is follow this teaching and treat illness in this way."

Baha'is are in touch with a spirit world.

"People who have died are able to get in touch with us. We can benefit from the love they give us. As they develop in wisdom, they try to give it to us. We have to be receptive to them, and to hear them."

Jehovah's Witnesses

Jehovah's Witnesses

Jehovah's Witnesses are members of the Watch Tower Bible and Tract Society. The Society was developed by two men: Charles Russell, and Judge Joseph Rutherford. Charles Taze Russell was born in Pittsburgh, USA in 1852. As he grew up he gradually rejected his parents' religion. When he was 18 years old, he met a group of Second Adventists. They were a group of people who believed that Jesus Christ would come back on earth in the near future, and that Christ's death had made it possible to enter the Kingdom of God. Russell shared these beliefs.

The Watch Tower movement

Russell was a rich young man, and he used his wealth to publish many free books and pamphlets about his beliefs. He encouraged people to read the Bible and said this would show them God's plan for the human race, including the return of Jesus. More and more people read his books, and so he formed the Watch Tower movement. He and his followers believed that Jesus would return to earth in 1914. This did not happen. Russell died in 1916, and his place as President of the Society was taken by Judge Joseph Rutherford, a forceful leader. He turned the movement into an organization which went out into the world to tell people about the Kingdom of God. In 1931 he announced that all members would have a name – Jehovah's Witnesses. The new name was to tell people that members of the movement had been specially chosen by God to 'bear witness' to their belief that Christ would soon return to earth.

The name Jehovah

Jehovah's Witnesses believe that the Bible is the direct word of God, and so everything said in it is literally true. The name 'God' is only a title; in the Bible God revealed his own personal name, 'Jehovah'. Witnesses do not see themselves as preaching from their own understanding. They believe they are pointing out what the Bible says, and honouring Jehovah by letting him speak. Jesus Christ is seen as Jehovah's son, but not of equal rank with Jehovah.

Everlasting life

Witnesses believe that the earth will last forever. All the people, both living and dead, who accept Jesus will live there. Heaven does exist and 144,000 chosen people, led by Jesus, will go there. They will form the Heavenly Kingdom which will look after those who live on the earth. Today such believers are being separated from the unbelievers, before this present system of things ends. Then the earth will become a place where everyone lives peacefully and happily.

The end of Satan

Witnesses believe that 'God's day' is equal to 1000 years, and that we are now in the period of time leading up to Judgement Day. The Heavenly Kingdom will soon come into being. Witnesses believe that Satan is a real spirit creature who creates evil in the world. For

Below: Charles Taze Russell, the founder of the Watch Tower Society. From the age of 11 he worked as a partner with his father in business. Together they built up a chain of shops which sold clothes. The money which he earned enabled him to begin the work of publishing his views on the Bible.

example, he misleads people with false religions. God has allowed both Satan and human beings to rebel from him. We all have a free will, and sometimes do things which are evil. Nevertheless, Jehovah notes those people who obey his laws. Satan knows he has only a short time left before he is destroyed.

Sin and death

Adam and Eve, whom the Bible tells were the first people God made, are seen as responsible for sin and death. They disobeyed God and were driven out from the peaceful world he made for them into our world, which is evil.

Jesus Christ's death, however, created forgiveness for this sin, and made it possible for the human race to take part in the 'World to Come'. The punishment given to the human race (who are Adam and Eve's descendants), has now almost come to an end. Witnesses believe that God has revealed this good news to them through the Bible.

The soul

Witnesses believe that body and soul are one. When the body dies, so does the soul. Death is a state of unconsciousness from which believers will awaken when Jesus comes again.

Above: Witnessing in action. For all Witnesses going out and talking to members of the public is one of the most important ways in which they can show their beliefs. Here a Witness in a small country town in Britain is discussing her faith with a non-Witness.

Jehovah's Witnesses
Not of the world

Witnesses obey Christ's statement to his disciples: 'My Kingdom is not part of this world.' They do not take part in politics, and refuse all military service. They do not salute flags or recognise national anthems. They also refuse to give or receive blood transfusions because of a sentence in the Bible which says 'You will not eat blood.' But they believe they should love each other, regardless of background or colour, and call one another 'brother' and 'sister'.

How the Society is organized

There are no clergy and each Witness is a 'minister'. Everyone, from the directors of the Society to the newest Witness, preaches from house to house. There are over six million Witnesses worldwide, and they conduct almost five million Bible studies a week (on average) in the homes of interested people. The Witnesses are governed by the President of the Society and the directors. Every congregation (local Witness group) has its Body of Elders, helped by Ministerial Servants. Their journal, *The Watch Tower*, is translated into 139 languages, with over 23 million copies printed twice a month. The companion magazine *Awake!* is published in 83 languages.

Theocratic Ministry School

Each congregation of Witnesses organizes its own school. There, Witnesses learn how to preach and contact the public. Witnesses spend many hours studying the Bible and Watch Tower publications, so that they can answer questions about them easily. They also go to five one-hour meetings each week in their local meeting place, which is always called 'Kingdom Hall'.

Baptism

Witnesses do not baptize babies or children. When a teenager is thought old enough to understand what baptism means and expresses a desire to take this step, or when a new person is converted, they are baptized. This involves the person's whole body being put under water for a few moments, and is called total immersion.

Children

Children in Jehovah's Witnesses families do not have birthday parties. This is because their parents believe that the early Christians did not celebrate birthdays. They also don't celebrate Christmas and Easter, since the Bible does not say that these should be religious festivals. Nor do children usually go to school dances, plays or clubs. Many Witnesses' children also do not always attend religious instruction classes in their schools. They believe that much that is taught doesn't follow the Bible accurately.

Below: A meeting in a Kingdom Hall. The speaker is helping Witnesses to understand the Bible. He explains a passage and asks questions to make sure he is understood. The piano in the background is used to accompany the singing of hymns. Each congregation has its own Kingdom Hall.

The meetings include sermons, giving advice, and question and answer sessions. Everyone who comes to the meetings is involved, including children.

Left: 181 people were baptized at this mass baptism in 1984. The Witnesses often hold large meetings in such places as sports grounds and stadiums. The Witnesses call this 'Kingdom Increase', because the numbers of Witnesses are being added to.

Below: The book centre at the British headquarters of the Watch Tower Society. Copies of the many books on Witness beliefs are sent from here to interested people in many countries and also to Kingdom Halls up and down the country. Many hundreds of thousands of copies of books are printed.

Misunderstandings

Witnesses are just 'Bible thumpers'.

"People think that we are the old-fashioned type of Bible thumpers and will thunder at them on their doorstep and preach hell-fire at them. We do not believe in that."

The Watch Tower movement does not welcome outsiders.

"Anyone can attend our meetings and the door is always open. Our work is not to keep anyone out, but to open people's hearts to Jehovah. In the Bible, Jehovah told us to go forth and teach and he would be with us always."

Witnesses' children lead very narrow lives.

"People say that our children lead dull lives, but we still give them presents even though we do not celebrate birthdays. It is not true, either, that our teenagers are too restricted. They are the same as adults, they obey the rules against the breaking of God's laws. It can be seen what happens to the teenagers who ignore those laws."

Hare Krishnas
Krishna, Krishna

Swami Prabhupada, the founder of the Hare Krishna movement, died in 1977. Before he left India in 1965 he had written just three books: in the next 12 years, living in the West, he wrote more than 60. Before he left India he had taught only one disciple: in the West he taught 4000 more. When he was 69 years old he left India for the first time: before he died he had travelled many times round the world.

George Harrison, who was a member of the famous British pop group, The Beatles, said o him: "The thing that always stays is his saying 'I am the servant of the servant of the servant.' I like that. A lot of people say, 'I'm it. I'm the divine incarnation.' But Prabhupada was neve like that. I liked Prabhupada's humbleness. I always liked his humility and his simplicity."

Waking up

The *Swami* was a Hindu with a message for th West. He taught what he saw as the need to 'wake up' to reality. He said that people often live as though they were dreaming, and that human beings have forgotten what they are really like. People have accepted a temporary physical body instead as if it was their true self The Hindu holy writings compare what it is like to be asleep and dreaming with being awake. When people sleep, they forget their waking selves. But when the alarm clock goes off people stop sleeping and wake up. Then they remember who they are and what they should be doing.

In the same way, when the powerful sound of the song which the members of the Hare Krishna movement sing is heard, a person is able to wake up. They can become aware of who they really are and that their soul is eterna and full of happiness. The goal in life, said the *Swami*, is for people to wake up like this, rathe than look for pleasure in the material world.

The mantra

Hare Krishnas believe that the easiest and bes way to awaken is to chant their special song, called a *mantra*, which contains the Hindu names of God. 'Krishna' is the most importan of God's names. When the *Swami* first chante the *mantra* in New York in 1965, many people were attracted to it, and to the *Swami*. They included musicians, poets and artists, and many who were on drugs. The drug addicts gave up drugs under the influence of the *mantra*. The movement grew and soon many people in New York and San Francisco were committed to chanting. Here is the mantra:

Hare Krishna, Hare Krishna
Krishna, Krishna, Hare, Hare
Hare Rama, Hare Rama
Rama, Rama, Hare, Hare

Chant and be happy

Rama is another name for God. The *Swami* taught that the names of God are as importan

Left: A shrine to the Indian god Krishna and his female partner, Radha. A Hare Krishna follower is placing a flower on the shrine, while others put their foreheads on the ground with hands together. This is their way of showing respect to Krishna and Radha. Hare Krishnas regard Krishna as a real god who once lived on earth.

as the holy writings themselves. The names can be sung aloud or meditated upon silently. He believed that they have within them God's complete spiritual power. God and his name are the same.

According to some Hindu teachers 'Krishna' is the most powerful name for God. It is said to bring blissful happiness when chanted by people. This is why it is part of the *mantra* which the *Swami* taught.

Reincarnation

Hare Krishnas believe that they are not just their bodies, but eternal spirit souls. As such they are all brothers and sisters and Krishna is their common father. Until they are fully woken up, they will be reincarnated – that is, they will return to this life time after time in a new body. They try to be peaceful and loving in this life so that their next birth will be full of love and happiness.

Hare Krishnas
The four principles

Hare Krishnas obey four rules of spiritual life. They believe these will help them to become less attached to their bodies:
- No eating of meat, fish or eggs.
- No drinking of alcohol, tea or coffee, and no drugs.
- No gambling.
- Sexual relationships should only take place within marriage, and then only in order to have children who will be brought up as God-centred.

What they do
The members of the Hare Krishna movement now have centres in many large cities. They go out every day in London, Paris, New York and other capital cities to make the *mantra* heard. They dance one behind the other in a long curving line. As they dance they chant the *mantra*, beat drums and shake hand cymbals. The men are dressed in flowing yellow robes and have shaven heads. The women wear colourful Indian saris. They believe that what they are doing helps others, and that it may also help them to wake up to who they really are.

Daily life
Full-time members of the movement get up early every morning to chant before they do their daily work. They hope to reach a state of

Right: A Hare Krishna follower taking part in a ceremony. The white mark on his forehead is a sign to others that he is a follower of Krishna. A fire burns at all Hare Krishna ceremonies, to purify the actions of those taking part in them.

mind which they call 'Krishna Consciousness' to help them during the day. They try to live in communities, and to meet together as often as possible. They believe that being with other people who share their views gives them spiritual strength. Nobody under the age of 16 is accepted as a new member of the movement, unless they have their parents' consent. But children who are born to members practise chanting from an early age. Many go to a special school in Paris. Whatever work a member does is done not for themselves, but for Krishna. Any food which a member of the movement eats is offered first to the Lord Krishna. Members believe that Krishna then becomes the food and purifies the person who eats it.

Study

Hare Krishnas believe that it is important to learn the Hindu scriptures, particularly the Bhagavad Gita, which the *Swami* has translated. They spend some time each day reading and discussing the scriptures with a teacher. They feel it is important that only someone who is unselfish and whose mind is firmly fixed on Krishna should teach.

Misunderstandings

Hare Krishnas brainwash their members.

"In a sense, any form of education or discipline is brainwashing. It depends on your standard. In the Hare Krishna movement, the teaching helps members to become healthy, clear-headed and sharply intelligent."

What Hare Krishnas teach is very different from Christianity.

"It is completely in keeping with what Jesus taught. But there seems to be a difference between his teaching and what the churches say. We believe that the soul-life in every creature is the same, so that there is no difference between the soul of a person and the soul of a pig."

Hare Krishna children do not go to state schools.

"We believe this would expose them to the misleading teaching of the state schools. The juniors go to a special primary school."

Above: A shrine containing an image of Krishna being carried through London, in a Hare Krishna procession. This is part of an ancient Indian festival known as Rathayatra ('festival of the chariot') when Krishna is carried in public so that everyone can see him.

Hare Krishnas now celebrate this festival all over the world. Swans are painted on the shrine because Hare Krishnas try to imitate this bird's grace and calm.

Left: Although they do not have to, some Hare Krishnas (like this boy) choose to shave off most of the hair on their heads. This is done as a sign of cleanliness and renunciation of the world.

Rajneeshis
The Bhagwan

Bhagwan Shree Rajneesh was the founder of the Rajneesh movement. He was an Indian, who was born in 1931 and died in 1990. He had a spiritual awakening when he was 23, after a long time of struggling for just such an experience. It came, however, when he had given up, feeling hopeless. He said: "The day the search stopped, the day I was not looking for something it started happening. A new energy arose out of nowhere...The day the effort came to an end, I also came to an end."

Rajneesh was very happy for a short time after this experience, and a new feeling of what being alive meant grew inside him as the years went on. He became a professor of philosophy at two Indian universities.

He also travelled and gave lectures which people found new and startling about the scriptures of all religions. He used many jokes to point out the spiritual nature of the things he talked about.

The beginning of the movement
As his reputation grew, Shree Rajneesh stopped his university teaching to give himself more time to talk to all the followers who had begun to gather around him. He told them that there was just one energy in the world, which he called 'bio-energy'.

The unusual meditations he taught his followers were designed to help them understand this energy. He also believed that the energy could be transmitted from himself to his followers when he touched their foreheads with his own thumb.

Bhagwan
By the early 1970s Shree Rajneesh had been given the title of *Bhagwan* (God or Supreme Lord) by his followers, who now numbered thousands, both Indian and Western. He established his community, called an *ashram*, at Poona in north-west India, and began writing many books.

The break with tradition
Rajneesh angered some Indians by telling his followers that they could become *sannyasins* (a Hindu religious word meaning recluse or monk). His followers took a new Indian name, and wore robes and clothes which were always

Below: *Bhagwan* Rajneesh greets some friends in New York, using the Indian palms-together form of greeting. The *Bhagwan* used to travel a lot and was always surrounded by groups of followers.

coloured orange and red. They carried a string of 108 prayer beads (which Hindus also carry), but with a locket attached which held Rajneesh's photograph. And instead of living away from the world as recluses, Rajneesh told them they should live life to the full.

Many Hindus wait for most of their lives before they become a *sannyasin* and wear an orange robe. But Rajneesh told his followers that they could wear the robe (which means rejection of the world) while still enjoying a full life. Also, each follower, however young and inexperienced, was given the title of *Swami*, which to Hindus has the meaning of a wise and well-trained teacher.

Eventually the hostility brought about by the way Rajneesh's followers lived may have caused the closure of the *ashram* in India. In 1981 the *Bhagwan* moved his *ashram* to Oregon in the USA.

The sannyasin's life

Rajneesh's *sannyasins* usually worked for 12 hours a day and called this work their worship. In Rajneeshpuram, the *Bhagwan's ashram* in the USA, they began to build a city. From time to time they stopped work to listen to a talk or attend a group meeting. Once a day, Rajneesh drove round the *ashram* in one of his many cars to wave to his followers.

Below: Rajneesh explains some of the principles of his beliefs to a large group of followers. The many varying shades of orange in the dress of his followers shows why they sometimes call themselves 'The Orange People'. The orange colour is part of the dress of the Hindu *sannyasin*.

Rajneeshis
Explosion

Rajneesh said that people all over the world had been trying for hundreds of years to ignore thir own suffering. He did not believe that anyone could take part in silent meditation without first letting go all the tensions that have built up in their minds and bodies. He said: "The calmness, the serenity, the bliss, comes not by stilling the mind, but by explosion."

How explosion is practised
Rajneesh called his technique 'Dynamic Meditation'. First, people breathe very rapidly. This builds up pressure in their bodies. Then the tension and pressure in the body is released in a kind of explosion of energy, when everybody does whatever they want. They may scream, cry, laugh, or jerk about. After some time doing this, they begin to shout the word 'Hoo!' They shout it as loudly as possible. This is said to knock out the blocked-up energy centres in their bodies, until the energy is completely released. Then everybody stands totally still and silent for a time, allowing the force of their released feelings to be felt inside them. Finally, everybody sings or dances and celebrates the relief and joy they are feeling.

How to live
Rajneesh believed that everybody should try out everything. He did not forbid any habit or practice to his followers. He said: "Don't live a repressed life, otherwise you do not live at all. Live a life of expression, creativity, joy. Live the way God wanted you to live; live the natural way. Listen to your instincts; listen to your body; listen to your heart; listen to your intelligence. Depend on yourself, and go wherever your spontaneity takes you. And you will never be at a loss. And going spontaneously with your natural life, one day you are bound to arrive at the doors of the divine."

Bringing up children
Rajneesh believed that families with only two parents were a bad thing. He believed that children should be brought up in communities of people of both sexes and all ages.

Hopes for the future
Rajneesh believed that after his death his teaching would become a religion. He wrote down many of his ideas, so that his followers would be able to read them. When he went to live in the United States, he began a period of silence, which is a custom in some Hindu traditions. He felt that because he had written so much, there was nothing more he needed to say.

Below: Rajneesh drives around the *ashram* at Rajneeshpuram blessing his followers. He used to do this once a day and all work stopped as he passed by. Everyone lined up to see the *Bhagwan* and make contact with him in this way.

Rajneeshis today

When the *Bhagwan* was alive there were around half a million Rajneeshis. Some famous film and music stars belonged to the movement. Rajneeshis always wore red and orange Indian-style clothes and both men and women usually had long hair.

The *Bhagwan* received many gifts from his followers and became a wealthy man. At one time he owned 72 expensive cars. In the 1980s his business affairs were investigated by the police and he was forced to leave Oregon. Since his death in 1990 the number of Rajneeshis has dwindled.

Above: The marriage of two Rajneeshis. A photograph of the *Bhagwan* can be seen in the background. The marriage is performed by a Rajneeshi teacher. The ceremony is informal. The teacher reads some words by the *Bhagwan* about love and marriage, and the couple exchange flowers. Afterwards, there is music and dancing.

Misunderstandings

Rajneesh cannot be a holy man and be so wealthy.

"It doesn't matter to me how many expensive cars or jewels Rajneesh has. All that is on the outside edge of what really matters. What's important is what is happening to me, inside myself. Rajneesh has helped me learn so much about myself. All he says and does is to help you know yourself and what you are."

Dynamic Meditation is so uncontrolled it could be harmful.

"That is not true. The feeling of letting go, when your whole body moves and when sound pours out in your voice, is a very healing experience."

Shouting 'Hoo' sounds a bit silly.

"'Hoo' is a holy word meaning God. The Sufis, who are Muslims, pray to God by calling 'Hoo'. We use that holy sound to blow blocked up feelings out of our minds."

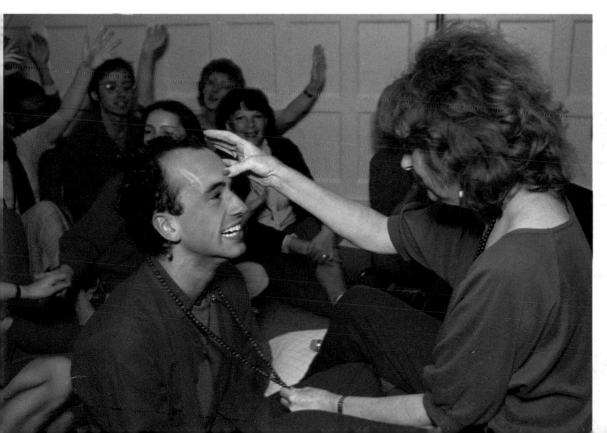

Left: A new convert becomes a *sannyasin* at a special ceremony. A Rajneesh official, wearing purple, presses her thumb on his forehead. This signifies the passing of sacred energy into the whole body of the new *sannyasin*.

Further information

A glossary of useful words

Note: these explanations of words are the ones used by the groups in this book.

ashram is an Indian word which means to guide or teach. An *ashram* is a place such as Rajneesh's where teaching takes place.

awakening Hare Krishnas believe that to awaken is to become aware of oneself in a new way.

Babylon a land which, in the Bible, belonged to the enemies of the Israelites. For Rastafarians it means the land of exile.

Bhagavad Gita a Hindu scripture which describes how the God Krishna helped Arjuna to win a war. It is studied by Hare Krishnas.

Bhagwan a Hindu title which means 'God', or 'Supreme Lord', given to Shree Rajneesh.

Christianity the religion based on the teaching of Jesus Christ. It is a false teaching to the Rastafarians because they believe Haile Selassie to have been the real Christ.

clergy people chosen to do special jobs in religious groups. The Baha'is do not have clergy or ministers because they believe each Baha'i is a teacher.

divine coming from God. Mormons believe that the plan for the human race which Joseph Smith rediscovered was a divine plan.

Divine Principle the Reverend Moon believes the Divine Principle which was revealed to him is how God governs the world.

exile to be forced to leave your own country and live in another. Rastafarians believe they are exiles from Africa.

fast to go without food. The Mormons fast on the first Sunday of every month.

'God's Day' Jehovah's Witnesses believe that a day in the eyes of God lasts for 1000 years.

guru a Hindu word meaning 'the remover of darkness'. He who removes darkness from a person's understanding is a *guru*, and the Maharishi Mahesh Yogi is called this.

Haile Selassie the Emperor of Ethiopia, crowned in 1930. Rastafarians believe he fulfilled a Biblical prophecy and was the son of God.

heaven a place where people whom God loves go when they die. Mormons believe they lived there before birth, and will return after death.

Heavenly Kingdom a part of heaven where, according to the Jehovah's Witnesses, 144,000 good people will go to look after those on earth.

Hebrew the old Israeli language in which Mormons believe the golden tablets revealed to Joseph Smith were written.

hell a place of punishment for disobeying religious laws.

Hindu a person who practices the main religion of India, such as *Swami* Prabhupada of the Hare Krishnas.

I-tal Rastafarians prepare their food in a pure and careful way which they call *I* (for God) – *tal* (for natural).

incarnation a spirit taking on a body. When a god enters the body of a person it is said to be the god's incarnation. Some religious leaders have claimed they are gods in this way.

Israelites God's chosen people in the Bible. Mormons believe that two of the 12 tribes of Israel came to South America 4000 years ago.

Jah the Rastafarian word for God. It is a new form of the Biblical name for God, Jehovah.

Jehovah the name used by Jehovah's Witnesses for God. They believe it is his personal name.

mantra a word or sound repeated in the mind. TM gives each follower a different sound. Hare Krishnas repeat names of God as a *mantra*.

meditation TM followers use their *mantra* to attain a state of mind called meditation, when the mind becomes still and clear.

Muslim a person who follows the teachings of the prophet Muhammad.

Nyabingi the name for an African protest movement led by Haile Selassie. The name is now given to large meetings of Rastafarians.

pilgrimage a journey made to show religious beliefs. The Baha'is travel to Mount Carmel in Israel as a place of pilgrimage.

prophet a person who foretells a future situation, or the coming of a great person. For Rastafarians, Marcus Garvey was a prophet who foretold the crowning of Haile Selassie.

Ras Tafari was the name of Haile Selassie. It means 'Prince of the House of Tafari'.

recluse a person who does not take part in ordinary life. Rajneesh does not want his followers to become recluses.

reggae Rastafarian music of drums and steel instruments. Famous groups are Steel Pulse, The Meditations and the Wailers.

reincarnation the return of a soul after death into another body. Members of four groups in this book believe this happens.

religious order a group of people who agree to follow certain religious ideals and who take a name such as Franciscans (Christianity).

samyama a way of meditation practised by

TM which is thought to bring about remarkable powers such as knowledge of previous lives.

sannyasin a person becomes a *sannyasin* in India when they decide not to take part in worldly affairs. They wear orange robes. The Rajneesh followers are called *sannyasins*.

scriptures the holy writings of a religion. The Hare Krishna movement studies the Hindu scriptures, particularly the Bhagavad Gita.

sect a part of a large religious group which does not share all the beliefs of the group. When Joseph Smith was growing up there were many Christian sects in America.

shrine a special place containing holy objects, such as the picture of a god. The Hare Krishnas create shrines around Krishna images.

sidhi an Indian word for an unusual power of the mind developed during meditation. In TM, rising above the ground is a *sidhi*.

soul a spirit which remains when the body dies. In the Baha'i faith the soul and the body are seen as being like a light and a mirror. When the body dies and the mirror is broken, the light continues to shine.

spiritual means to be concerned with the spirit, or soul. Most religions are spiritual.

spiritual healers people who believe that the power of God or some other non-physical force helps to heal the sick, as in the Baha'i faith.

Swami the Indian title for a revered spiritual teacher. The founder of the Hare Krishnas was called a *Swami*.

total immersion people are baptized as Mormons or Jehovah's witnesses by being dipped completely under water.

transcendent beyond the range of the universe. In TM transcendent meditation means a meditation which goes beyond everyday experiences.

translate the scriptures which Joseph Smith discovered written on gold plates were in Hebrew. He had to translate them into English before they could be understood by the people around him, who did not know Hebrew.

Tribes of Israel the Bible teaches that there were once 12 tribes of Israeli people, who became separated. Mormons believe that two of the tribes went to South America.

vision seeing a spiritual being, such as God.

witness to speak about God and the Bible believing it to be the factual truth. This is what Jehovah's Witnesses do when they call on people in their homes.

Books for further reading

Books suitable for young readers on these religions are hard to find. The books listed below are for older readers and teachers.

Mormons
Inside the Mind of Joseph Smith Robert D. Anderson (Signature Books, 1999)
As a Thief in the Night: The Mormon Quest for Millennial Deliverance Dan Erickson (Signature Books, 1998)
American Prophet: The Story of Joseph Smith Heidi S. Swinton (Shadow Mountain Press, 1999)

Rastafarians
The Rastafarians Leonard E. Barrett (Beacon Press, 1997)
Yes Rasta Patrick Cariou and Perry Henzell (Powerhouse Books, 2000)
A Rasta's Pilgrimage Neville Garrick (Pomegranate Paperbacks, 1999)
The Kebra Negast: the Book of Rastafarian Wisdom and Faith from Ethiopia to Jamaica Gerald Hausman (ed.) (St Martin's Press, 1997)
Chanting Down Babylon: The Rastafari Reader Nathaniel Samuel Murrell (ed.) (Temple University Press, 1998)
Dread Jesus William Spencer (SPCK, 1999)

Unification Church
Messiah Bo Hi Pak (University Press of America, 2001)
Studies in Contemporary Religion: The Unification Church Massimo Introvigne (Signature Books, 2000)
Science and Absolute Values: Twenty Addresses Sun Myung Moon (Icus Books, 1997)

Transcendental Meditation
Ageless Body, Timeless Mind: The Quantum Alternative to Growing Old Deepak M.D. Chopra (Three Rivers Publishing, 1998)
Creating Health: How to Wake Up the Body's Intelligence Deepak M.D. Chopra (Houghton Mifflin Co, 1999)
Science of Being and Art of Living: Transcendental Meditation Mahesh Yogi et al (Meridian Books, 1994)

Baha'i Faith
Who is Writing the Future? The Baha'i
International Community Office of Public
Information (Baha'i Publication Trust, 2000)
Modernity and the Millennium Juan Ricardo Cole
(Columbia University Press, 1998)
The Elements of the Baha'i Faith Joseph
Sheppherd (Element Books, 1997)
A Concise Encyclopaedia of the Baha'i Faith Peter
Smith (Oneworld Publications, 1997)

Jehovah's Witnesses
Jehovah's Witnesses in the Twentieth Century
Questions Young People Ask – Answers that Work
Mankind's Search for God
  These titles plus the magazines *The Watch
Tower* and *Awake!* are distributed by the
Watchtower Bible and Tract Society of
Pennsylvania and are available in the UK from
Kingdom Halls.

Hare Krishnas
Fortunate Souls Danavir Dasa Goswami and
Dane Holtzman (Rupanuga Vedic College,
1996)
*Every Day Just Right: Welcome Home to the One
Big Book of Your Life* Satsvarupa Dasa Gosvami
(Gita Nagari, 1998)
Hinduism, TM and Hare Krishna J. Isamu
Yamamoto et al (Zondervan Publishing, 1998)

Rajneeshis
Courage: The Joy of Living Dangerously Osho
(Griffin Paperbacks, 1999)
*The Mustard Seed: Commentaries on the Fifth
Gospel of St Thomas* Osho and Osho Rajneesh
(Element Books, 2000)
No Water, No Moon: Talks on Zen Stories Osho,
Osho Rajneesh (Element Books, 2000)

Websites

http://www.paston.co.uk/users/bcreak/mormon
Information about the Mormons.

http://www.swagga.com
Information about Rastafarianism.

http://www.unification.net/
The homepage for the Unification Church.

http://www.t-m.org.uk
For information about learning TM anywhere in
the UK.

http://www.baha'i.org
Information about the Baha'i faith.

http://www.watchtower.org
The homepage for the Jehovah's Witnesses.

http://www.harekrishna.com/
The homepage for Hare Krishnas.

Addresses

Mormons
Public Communications Department
The Church of Jesus Christ of Latter-Day Saints
64-68 Exhibition Road
London SW7 2PA

Unification Church
Information Department
Unification Church
43 Lancaster Gate
London W2 3NA

Baha'is
National Spiritual Assembly of the Baha'i Faith
27 Rutland Gate
London SW7 1PD

Christian Science
126 New Kings Road
London SW6

Church of Scientology
68 Tottenham Court Road
London W1P

Index

Numbers in heavy type refer to picture captions, or to the pictures themselves.

Illustration Credits

Key to positions of illustrations: (T) top, (L) left, (B) bottom, (R) right

Photographic sources
Camerapix Hutchison Library: 13, 40, 41T
Camera Press: cover (BR), 36
Bruce Coleman Ltd.: cover (T)
Church of Jesus Christ of Latter-Day Saints: 11, 12T, 12B
Daily Telegraph Colour Library: contents page, 14, 17T, 37B
Richard and Sally Greenhill: cover (TC)
Robert Harding Picture Library: cover (LC), 10
Impact Photos:/Colin Jones: 15
David Reed: title page, 35, 41B
International Cultural Foundation: 18T
National Spiritual Assembly of the Baha'i Faith: 26, 27, 28, 29T, 29B
Popperfoto: 8(R)
Bury Peerless: endpapers, 3, 37T
Rex Features: cover (BL), 8(L), 9, 17B, 18B, 22B, 25, 34, 38, 38–39
Homer Sykes: 16
Watch Tower Bible and Tract Society: 30, 31, 32, 33T, 33B